A Rainbow of Parrots

THE WILY LIFE OF A FEATHERED GENIUS

BY VICKI LEÓN

LONDON TOWN PRESS

The London Town *Wild Life* Series
Series Editor
Vicki León

A Rainbow of Parrots
Principal photographer
Clayton Fogle

Additional photographers
R.H. Armstrong; Stanley Breeden; Dr. Donald Brightsmith;
Jane Burton; John Chellman; Ralph A. Clevenger; E.R.
Degginger; Michael Dick; Richard R. Hansen; Noah Hawthorne;
R.F. Head; Kevin Horan; M.P. Kahl; Zig Leszczynski; Tom
Mangelsen; C. Allan Morgan; Oxford Scientific Films; Robert
Pearcy; Fritz Prenzel; George Schaller; Stan Thompson; Rod
Williams; Art Wolfe; Belinda Wright

London Town Press
P.O. Box 585
Montrose, California 91021
www.LondonTownPress.com

Book design by Christy Hale
10 9 8 7 6 5 4 3 2 1

Printed in Singapore

Distributed by Publishers Group West

Publisher's Cataloging-in-Publication Data
León, Vicki.
A rainbow of parrots : subtitle goes here / Vicki León;
photographs by Clayton Fogle [et al.] —2nd ed.
p. cm. — (London Town wild life series)
Originally published: San Luis Obispo, CA : Blake Books ©1990.
Summary: Describes the behaviors, habitats and life cycles of
parrots, cockatoos and macaws, with full-color photographs.
Includes bibliographic references and index.
ISBN 0-9766134-2-5
1. Parrots—Juvenile literature. 2. Macaws—Juvenile literature.
3. Cockatoos—Juvenile literature. [1. Parrots. 2. Macaws.
3. Cockatoos.] I. Fogle, Clayton II. Title. Series.
QL696.P7 L46 2005
598.71—dc22
2005930187

In the captions and index of this book, each parrot is called
by the common name used by ornithologists, followed by its
scientific name.

FRONT COVER: Blue and yellow macaws (*Ara ararauna*) spend
hours grooming each other. They carefully clean each feather.
When these birds get excited, the white skin on their faces
sometimes turns pink.

TITLE PAGE: A pink cockatoo (*Cacatua leadbeateri*) wears a
fancy headdress that looks like the war-bonnet of a Native
American chief. A near-threatened species, it feeds on
pinecone seeds and figs, often in the company of galahs and
corellas. When courting, both birds bow, raise their crests and
chatter softly.

BACK COVER: Cockatoos like this sulfur-crested beauty
(*Cacatua galerita*) from Australia and the South Pacific roost
in pairs. To feed, they climb around trees, eating hawthorn
berries, flowers, and insect larvae. In flocks, they also move
across the ground to find roots and grass seeds. To spot danger,
one bird will keep watch while the other cockatoos eat.

Contents

The secret life of a wild and wily bird

*A*t four o'clock in the morning, it's cool and dark as I slog through muddy water and jungle vegetation. I'm deep in the rainforests of Peru, on my way to one of the world's wonders—a cliff at the river's edge called a clay lick.

Parrots, like human beings, crave salt. I'm here to learn how parrot species, especially the magnificent macaws, find their secret supply—and in the process, how they live their wild lives.

I'm one of twelve Earthwatch volunteers helping an American scientist do research here. We don't talk. Instead, as the sky lightens, we stand opposite the cliff of clay and scan the tall ironwood trees along the skyline with our binoculars.

▶ A mated pair of scarlet macaws *(Ara macao)* fly in perfect harmony through their Peruvian rainforest home. Macaws are powerful fliers with long tail feathers like colorful streamers.

I hear loud rough cries. "Scarlet macaws," someone whispers, and we make notes. Two macaws fly over us, their wings huge against the sky.

Suddenly birds approach from all directions. In noisy bands, the mealy Amazon parrots fly in. More macaws arrive and land on the treetops, their bodies splashed with color-crayon reds and blues, yellows and greens. Birds already in the trees snarl at them. Smaller parrots and mini macaw species paint the sky with more color and chatter.

As we watch, birds begin to leave the trees. Some circle in flocks, vocalizing nonstop. The small macaws cut in and out, showing the others how it's done. Human researchers call this behavior "the dance."

◄ Each morning at this clay lick in the Peruvian rainforest, scarlet macaws *(Ara macao)* and other parrots do a circular "dance" around the area, finally landing on the clay soil when they are sure it is safe from predators. The camera's stop action catches the beautiful wing and tail movements of these superb fliers.

The number grows to hundreds of birds and a dozen species. As they circle, the birds skim past the clay lick but don't touch down. Finally, just as the sun appears, the first bird dares to land on the clay. It's a red-bellied macaw.

The racket from the parrots goes up a notch, as if the birds are cheering. Ten mealy Amazons, their green feathers gleaming like metal, drop to the lick and begin feeding. Two pairs of blue and yellow macaws follow.

Just then, I get my first lesson about parrot survival in the wild. A vulture flies over the area. It's a scavenger, not a predator. Nevertheless, all the parrots bolt away, shrieking alarms as they fly. As the big macaws whizz over my head, I see they

▶ On the vertical cliffs beside the Tambopata River, hundreds of birds gather at this clay lick. Light green Amazon mealy parrots (*Amazona farinosa*) cuddle while eating their daily ration of clay; they are aptly called a huddle species. Near the mealy parrots, larger blue and yellow macaws (*Ara ararauna*) come and go, some carrying clay away in their beaks.

still carry chunks of clay in their huge beaks.

Parrots dislike all surprises, even harmless ones; no wonder these wary birds live a long time.

In silence, we Earthwatchers wait. By cautious ones and twos, the macaws venture back to the lick. Smaller parrots return to zinging round the area, and the noisy action builds.

By six o'clock, the vertical wall of reddish-brown clay is splashed with living color. Blue-headed parrots cluster. Above them, scarlet macaws chew clay. Our mechanical pencils move fast, noting the arrival of new species: orange-cheeked parrots, white-eyed parakeets, and two chestnut-fronted macaws.

Over 17 species of macaws and parrots come to this particular clay lick, one of many licks throughout the rainforest and elsewhere in the world. The birds get the salt they need from the clay, which also seems to protect them from toxins in the seeds and unripe fruits they eat.

During breeding season and the months when food supplies are most plentiful, these birds make daily visits to the lick. Only a downpour keeps the macaws away; they don't like getting soaked. I enjoy that fact; it's something I share with the macaws.

I begin to see what "mated for life" means to a parrot. The big macaws tend to go

everywhere in pairs. When they've finished eating clay, they sit side by side in treetops. They forage for food, muttering in croaky voices as they crack nuts. Afterwards, they play endlessly, one macaw dangling upside down while the other teases.

They even fly together. Each morning in the Tambopata reserve of Peru, countless pairs of macaws sail across their freshly washed rainforest world. I hope that every morning can be like this one for these glorious birds, and those who love them.

From topknot to tailfeathers

▲ An Australian king parrot (*Alisterus scapularis*) moves through the forest canopy in Bunya National Park, feeding on berries, mistletoe, and insect larvae. The glossy red-headed male courts its green-headed mate by head-bobbing and mutual feeding.

In a general sense, the word "parrot" refers to the 356 known species in this order of birds, which includes macaws, cockatoos, lories, lorikeets, true parrots, parrotlets, and parakeets. Almost all members of this diverse group are intelligent, curious, and social. A few species wear drab feathers but most boast colors that out-dazzle the rainbow.

During the millions of years that parrots have been around, a few hardy species have adapted to colder climates. The Austral parakeet braves the icy tip of

◀ Sulfur-crested cockatoos (*Cacatua galerita*) live in eastern Australia and on New Guinea and other South Pacific islands. When they feel alarmed or curious, their head feathers open like yellow fans. Females have lighter irises than the black-eyed males. Otherwise, adult birds look the same.

South America; the kea romps on the snowy slopes of New Zealand mountains. But most species prefer warmer places: Australia, South America, Central America, and parts of Africa and India. Parrots today brighten six continents and islands from the South Pacific to the Caribbean.

These remarkable birds come in all sizes. The pygmy parrot weighs less than half an ounce and is only four inches long. The big guy among parrots is the hyacinth macaw, which may reach 40 inches from beak to tail tip. A six-pound oddity called the kakapo is the heaviest—and the only parrot that cannot fly.

▲ No bigger than a golf ball at birth, a blue and yellow macaw (*Ara ararauna*) will become a three-foot-long adult. Cracking open nuts is a cinch for this macaw. It uses its powerful bill and agile claw-tipped toes to hold them.

► The yellow-shouldered Amazon parrot (*Amazona barbadensis*) is found only on Venezuela's coast and nearby islands. It eats cactus fruits, seed pods, and blossoms, bringing them to its mouth with one foot. Its toes can grip a slippery piece of fruit with ease. Because this handsome parrot is a favorite in the pet trade, its survival is threatened.

Large or small, parrots have superb tools to help them climb and forage. The upper and lower parts of a parrot's bill fit together as neatly as a jigsaw puzzle. Palm cockatoos and macaws have massive bills, able to crush rock-hard nuts with up to 500 pounds of pressure per square inch. Smaller birds like cockatiels use tiny pointed bills to harvest seeds.

To reach fruit, a parrot uses its bill and its feet. To climb treetrunks, a parrot uses its bill like a mountain climber uses an ice-axe. Most of these avian acrobats can grab, open, and turn tiny objects as well as a monkey.

Parrot feet are zygodactylous, a tongue-twister word that means two toes face forward and two face the other way. This adaptation lets each foot grip tightly. The hanging parrot carries this to extremes. At night, it dangles upside down by its feet to roost.

Short legs give parrots a waddling gait. When they walk, the feet of parrots turn in, giving them "pigeon toes." (Strangely enough, pigeons don't have them!) Another marvel is the parrot's busy tongue, as plump and inquisitive as a toddler's fingers. Like young children, parrots use their tongues to explore their world.

All parrots have color vision and see keenly. They often cock their heads to peer at something; this focuses their fovea, an area packed with vision cells. Researchers believe that parrots can also see in the ultraviolet range. The feathers of some species, including the cockatoo, rosella, grass parrot, golden conure, and budgerigar, carry a pigment that glows bright yellow in ultraviolet light. These fluorescent feathers may play a role in courtship displays.

▼ On a clay-filled cliff, two scarlet macaws *(Ara macao)* defend a favored spot against another mated pair of macaw-come-latelies. This clay lick, located on a river in the Tambopata Reserve of Peru, hosts hundreds of parrots and dozens of species each day.

Parrots are a huddle species, a term that describes their love of closeness. In the wild, most species do almost everything together. They forage in flocks. They fly in pairs, wingtips almost touching. They cuddle to preen, they play in noisy groups, they roost side by side.

This doesn't mean they are always peaceful. Parrots squabble and bite and get into fights. During breeding season, even flocking species like parakeets need space

and will pair off in twos. Mated pairs don't always get along, either.

Play is a key part of parrot social interaction. Macaws, for example, have lots of leisure time. Two by two, they swing from trees, engage in mock battles, and make lots of racket.

Most parrot species are wanderers that follow the seasonal availability of their food supply. Lories and other species may fly long distances to find food. Other species travel to breed, such as the swift parrot and the blue-winged parrot.

No matter where they roam, most parrots spend the night in roosting trees, safe from predators. At dawn, they leave for the day to search for food. At breeding time, most species roost with their mates, not the group.

Parrots have fewer feathers than other bird species. To keep their feathers airworthy and parasite free, they bathe often. Some make use of rainstorms, spreading their wings and tails to catch the drops. Macaws, however, tend to look for cover in a downpour.

Parrots also find bathing opportunities high in rainforest trees, where water collects in the foliage. In drier places like Australia, flocks of corellas and parakeets

▲ Sun conures *(Aratinga solstitalis)* live in northeastern parts of South America. They move in small flocks from tree to tree, eating ripening fruit, berries, and flowers. Most species of conures spend much time in pairs, grooming each other. Besides getting rid of parasites, this activity creates an emotional bond between the birds.

seek out waterholes. If fresh water is absent, parrots make do with dust baths.

Grooming or preening is an important activity, and not just to remove parasites. All parrots molt each year. When new feathers grow in, they're covered with an itchy layer. Birds spend hours preening each other to reduce the discomfort. It's a tender and painstaking act. A cockatoo will even groom around the eyes of its mate.

Despite its agile toes and bill, a parrot can't reach all its own body parts. A parrot will ask its mate for grooming by lowering its head. Among cockatoo species, one invites another by raising its crest. Parrots use their beaks and special oil glands to make their feathers glossy. Cockatoos also produce powder down, a special dust that conditions their feathers.

Wild parrots are basically vegetarians,

◄ Blue-headed rainbow lorikeets
(Trichoglossus haematodus)
and scaly-breasted lorikeets
(Trichoglossus chlorolepidotus)
love to bathe. Here, they use the
birdbath of a friendly Australian.
All parrots need to clean their
feathers. For bathtubs, they use
waterfalls, wet leaves, and raindrops.
While feeding, rainbow lorikeets
flock to their favorite trees, covering
them like Christmas ornaments.

and most live where the plants they feed
on bloom and ripen at different times.
They spend most of their time in trees,
eating what's found there: seeds, nuts,
fruits, buds, berries, and flowers.
Generalists, like some of the macaws
and the Amazon species, may feast on
hundreds of trees and plants.

Other parrots specialize. Lories and
lorikeets have brushy tongues that let

them lap up soft, liquid foods, like flower nectar and tree pollen. A couple of Andean parrot species live on mistletoe seeds. The hyacinth macaw sticks to crunchy, oil-rich palm nuts. Lovebirds gather grass seeds. Cockatiels feed in flocks, picking up acacia seeds from the ground as they wander.

A few parrots eat meat; rosellas go after grubs in treetrunks, while keas munch insects with their vegetables.

Farmers in Australia and elsewhere sometimes view parrots as pests, when cockatoos, rosellas, and other parrots feed on grain, fruit, or young coconuts. But many species also help farmers by eating the seeds of countless weeds.

Macaws only spend a few hours a day foraging. They work fast, creating a mess that would make your mother shake her head. After a macaw grabs a ripe fruit, it rips it open to get to the seeds, tossing the rest away. The fruit doesn't go to waste, though. On the ground below, peccaries (a type of jungle pig), lizards, and other creatures make quick work of it.

◄ High in a Central American forest, a female white-fronted Amazon parrot (*Amazona albifrons*) uses her bill and talented tongue to pluck a piece of fruit. She may be after the seeds inside. Although over 14 Amazon species are threatened with extinction, only a handful have been well studied.

▼ When eucalyptus trees begin to blossom in Australia, the musk lorikeet (*Glossopsitta concinna*) and other lory species come to eat and drink. In minutes, a flock of lorikeets can drink all the nectar from an entire flowering tree.

Nearly all parrots, macaws included, are called seed predators. That means they digest the seeds they eat. Bats and monkeys, on the other hand, pass seeds whole through their intestines and disperse them with their waste, but parrots do not.

Over time, jungle plants have developed ways to defend themselves by covering their seeds with very hard shells, then loading them with poisons to make them inedible. Still, most parrots manage to outwit the plants. With their strong beaks, they smash the shells and eat the bitter seeds anyway.

Some parrot species are born with a naturally high resistance to the chemical warfare of the plants they eat. Macaws, cockatoos, and African Grey parrots use another strategy. Between meals, they visit a clay lick. The salty clay helps neutralize the poisons in the seeds and plants they've just eaten.

▲ A scaly-breasted lorikeet (*Trichoglossus chlorolepidotus*) lives on dusty pollen and nectar, gathering them with a bumpy, brushy tongue. This fearless bird feeds on trees growing in cities as well as in the Australian countryside.

◀ In Australia, large flocks of these rosy birds, called galahs (*Cacatua roseicapillus*), drink water after feeding. A member of the cockatoo family, the galah also raises its head feathers into a crest when excited.

▲ Eclectus parrot males and females (*Eclectus roratus*) were once thought to be separate species. That's how different they look. The female's feathers go from rosy-red to purple. Her bill is black. The orange-billed male sports lime-green feathers. Their bright feathers have a furry quality.

A noisy, colorful family tree

Among birds in general, males are often showy, females are drab. Not so with parrots, where females also wear finery. The female eclectus parrot sports ruby-red plumage, trimmed with orange and purple-blue. Her mate has lime-green feathers, so the two look like Christmas all year round.

The most brilliant parrots may be the 50-plus species of lories and lorikeets. Their bodies shimmer in colors of shocking pink, orange, purple, electric blue and acid green, made brighter by the high gloss on their feathers.

Why do parrots wear such striking colors? Strangely enough, one reason is to hide. The rainforest where most parrots live is green, with big showy flowers and fruit. A flock of parrots can melt into these surroundings.

Vivid feathers and bright bills serve to attract mates and scare away rivals. Color is used to warn other birds, too. Traffic-signal colors, like red and yellow, are often found on a prominent part of the parrot's body, like its shoulders. When an Amazon parrot ruffles its feathers and leans forward, the message is clear: "Go away!" Parrots

▼ A native of Australia, the crimson-winged parakeet *(Apromictus erythropterus)* flies in large flocks to flowering trees. The rich color of its glossy feathers shows why parrots are so admired and sought after.

▲ Emotions are easy to read among cockatoos. The salmon-crested cockatoo (*Cacatua moluccensis*) spreads its head crest and fluffs its feathers to double its size. This behavior warns rivals to stay away from its mate. In the wild, this lovely bird is disappearing fast because too many have been captured for the pet trade.

also threaten by puffing their neck and crown feathers to appear bigger—and more colorful.

Not all parrots wear gaudy colors. There are coal-black lories and brown New Zealand parrots. Cockatoos wear soft plumes of white, black, or pink but steal the show with their headdress crests that open and close like fans.

Parrots are good at communicating with their bodies. Lorikeets are masters of intimidation; scientists have identified 30 of their threat gestures over food, nesting spots, and perches. Threat displays are ways of avoiding actual combat.

Skin and eyes are also used to warn or express excitement. Birds like the military macaw have areas of bare skin called cheek patches. They can blush with emotion, like we do. When excited, a number of parrot species also rapidly expand and contract their irises. This behavior is called eye-blazing. At times, courting parrots eye-blaze each other.

In the wild, parrots vocalize often, especially to warn each other of threats. For

▼ In isolated areas from Mexico to Argentina, the military macaw (*Ara militaris*) lives in pine trees or cloud forests. Like two other macaw species, it has feathered patterns on its cheek patches. As the photo shows, this macaw feels emotion. When it does, its cheek patches turn pink.

▶Big flocks of little corellas *(Cacatua sanguinea)* are a common sight in Australia. Strong fliers, these birds go far to find seeds, roots, insects, blossoms, and grasses. They have a more musical cry than some parrots. One of their vocalizations sounds like a creaky door.

▲ Parrots are loud and vocal, and the eclectus parrot *(Eclectus roratus)* is no exception. This male gives a raspy shriek. Using its hooked beak like a third hand, this South Pacific native climbs to its nest, high in a tree.

example, when cockatoos and other species eat in groups, one bird acts as a sentinel. If it senses danger, it gives a piercing alarm cry. Birds take turns serving as sentinel.

Wild parrots also murmur to their mates, caw to keep in contact while flying, and scream to point out food to the flock. In fact, the only times parrots keep quiet are when sleeping and when tending their nests and chicks.

Although wild parrots make many noises, these sounds do not resemble human speech. In the wild, African Grey parrots and Australian galahs sometimes imitate the calls of other birds and animals. So far, no other wild parrots have been documented doing the same.

Scientists have studied how parrots connect with each other. To bond with their mates, wild parrots use various patterns of vocalization, called duets. If they become pets, these intelligent birds try to socialize any way they can, even if that means learning to say "Polly want a cracker!" If it has no mate, a captive parrot will try to bond with its human owners.

►Little corellas (*Cacatua sanguinea*) love to play. Mated pairs often act like acrobats, hanging upside down—even rolling on their backs. Their sculpted white feathers and head crests show that they belong to the cockatoo family.

▼ For many years, Dr. Irene Pepperberg has been working with Alex, this Grey parrot *(Psittacus erithacus)*. Alex now has a very big vocabulary. Dr. Pepperberg's study has changed scientific beliefs. She has shown that a parrot's thinking and language abilities are equal to a dolphin or gorilla's.

In captivity, a number of species learn to talk, including parakeets, corellas, cockatiels, macaws, various Amazon parrot species, and African Grey parrots.

The Alexandrine ring-necked parakeet was the talking bird that long ago amazed the armies of Alexander the Great. Native to India, Africa, and southeast Asia, it lives in large flocks, feasting on ripe fruit.

The little corella, a smaller cockatoo, has a melodious cry and makes a creaky-hinge noise in the wild. Flocks of corellas are a common sight in Australia. As a pet, it mimics the human voice better than other cockatoo species.

Amazon parrots are smart, talkative birds with chunky green bodies. They range over much of South and Central America and the islands of the Caribbean.

Far and away the best talker is the African Grey parrot, a slim bird with wise

◀ Africa's largest parrot, the Grey parrot *(Psittacus erithacus)* eats cola nuts, seeds, and fruits. When it goes to roost at dusk, it travels to trees that may hold up to 10,000 birds. In the wild, the Grey parrot mimics other birds and animals. In captivity, it copies human speech and sound effects very well. To handle food, parrots like the Grey prefer one foot over another, just as human beings are left- or right-handed.

eyes and a brilliant scarlet tail. Other parrots mimic human speech, but the African Grey sounds uncannily human. It's been known to put together sentences, make up words, whisper, laugh, and sing. The Grey's ability to make the wildest, weirdest sound effects, from finger snapping to rude noises, is unsurpassed.

A keen brain goes with these talents. In long term studies with four parrots, including nearly 30 years with a Grey parrot named Alex, ethologist Dr. Irene Pepperberg has made groundbreaking discoveries. She has proven that Alex has the language skills of a child about two, and the ability to solve problems nearly as well as a child of five! This bird processes information, forms concepts, makes decisions, and remembers as well as primates and dolphins do.

Parrots lack a neocortex, the part of the brain long believed to be necessary for thought. So how do African Greys perform these cognitive feats? Diana May and Spencer Lynn, graduate students of Dr. Pepperberg, have studied Grey parrot societies in the wild. They believe that the complex society the Greys live in, combined with their long lifespans, have caused the birds to evolve in the direction of high intelligence and thinking ability. Other researchers have confirmed that parrot brains contain areas similar to the neocortex of mammals.

Dr. Pepperberg's work makes it clear why it's important and humane for pet parrots to get mental challenges and social stimulation. Her discoveries may also make human lives better. Her colleague Dr. Diane Sherman has adapted Dr. Pepperberg's training techniques to improve how autistic children are taught.

Borrowed homes, indulgent parents

Like other birds, parrots were once thought to mate for life. It's true that most do. But field studies have shown that species from conures to macaws may change mates for a variety of reasons.

These cautious birds can be surprisingly casual about nest sites, too. Many parrots simply borrow another creature's nest, burrow, or home. Fifteen percent of all species, including the pygmy parrot and the orange-fronted parakeet, nest inside termite mounds.

Whatever the site, parrot parents generally chew the entrance holes and interiors to make a safe place for their shiny white eggs.

Born blind, helpless, and naked, chicks make a shocking contrast to their sleek parents. As the weeks pass, their eyes open and pinfeathers sprout. Soon it's hard to believe they once looked like wads of pink bubble-gum. By the time chicks fledge and leave the nest, they look much like their parents.

Parrot ways of courting and chick rearing are as distinctive as the birds are.

◄ The orange-fronted conure (*Aratinga canicularis*) ranges from Mexico to Costa Rica. It eats figs, flowers, and the seeds of the kapok tree. It will nest in a cactus hollow but prefers termite mounds. When a parrot moves in with termites, the insects build a privacy wall between themselves and the bird.

Lovebirds of Africa and the island of Madagascar live up to their name by grooming one another in the most delicate fashion. During the breeding season, they also courtship feed, a loving but far from delicate activity. One bird fills its crop or throat pouch with food, then returns to its mate. The two birds get a grip on each others' heads and pump away. The stored food flows from the crop of one into the mouth of the other.

Although lovebird couples shower affection on each other, "love" is in short supply when it comes to other birds. During mating season, lovebirds get very aggressive. A lovebird will fence with its bill, beat its wings, and even put its feet against the chest of its rival.

The eight species of lovebirds reuse other birds' nests, but also build their own. The peach-faced lovebird carries building materials by tucking them into its rump

◄ In Africa there are eight species of lovebirds, including this peach-faced lovebird *(Agapornis roseicollis).* They form mated pairs, showing strong affection for each other. To make her nest, the female may carry bark strips or leaves, tucked into the feathers on her rump.

feathers. The Nyasa lovebird makes an impressive structure: a domed nest with an entrance tube, assembled by the female with bark strips and twigs.

Cockatoos are known for elaborate courtships. Male cockatoos strut and weave their heads from side to side in a figure-eight motion. Some species display in groups, or hang upside-down while raising their head crests. Once a female is won over, the two touch bills and preen each

▼ With care, a salmon-crested cockatoo (*Cacatua moluccensis*) preens the head feathers of its mate. Cockatoos produce a special powder that they rub into their plumage, making it extra soft and shiny. These birds sit at the opening of their nest hole in a palm tree. Soon the cockatoos will raise a new family.

◄ The Australian bluebonnet parrot (*Northiella haematogaster*) may raise two to four chicks. Like other parrots, this female feeds her chicks by regurgitating softened food from her crop. The crop in her throat acts as a pocket to carry acacia seeds, berries, and other foods.

► Two red and green macaws (*Ara chloroptera*) wake up from a nap. Often they mate for life. Ranging from Panama to Argentina, this spectacular bird looks a lot like the scarlet macaw. But look closer: this macaw has green on its wings, a blue tail-tip, and red patterns on its cheek patches.

other, while the male murmurs softly.

For nearly a month, cockatoo parents take turns warming the eggs, hidden in a palm tree or a cliff hole. Once hatched, the floppy chick is fed from the crops of the parents for nearly 40 days, until it can lift food with its own feet. As it grows, the chick's feet, tongue, and beak turn from pink to shiny black.

The world's most popular pet parrot was once hunted by the indigenous people of Australia. They named it budgerigar, or "pretty good eating." These small nomads still wander in flocks, seeking water and grass seeds. When they reach an area of recent rainfall, budgies breed, often mating a second time if rain falls again. Nesting in trees and burrows, they produce three to

five eggs per clutch. If weather permits, these chicks can hatch, mature, mate, and produce broods of their own within six months.

Australian cockatiels are slender, down-sized versions of cockatoos. They lay three to eight almond-sized eggs in the hollows of eucalyptus trees.

Natives of South America and Mexico, parrotlets are green charmers with short tails. They often nest in hollow trees or borrow other birds' nests. The bolder spectacled parrotlet may lay its eggs closer to the ground, using fencepost holes.

A prolific breeder, the monk parakeet nests and sleeps in colonies, throwing together untidy, condo-style bundles of sticks. Although from South America, this

◄ A scarlet macaw *(Ara macao)* prepares for sleep by tucking its head into its back feathers. It has no patterns on its cheek patches—the only large macaw without them. Found from Mexico to Brazil, scarlets are slow to breed and have a hard time finding good nesting sites. In South America, scientists work to increase their breeding success and to help more of their chicks survive.

bird is hardy enough to survive winters in the Midwest and has established populations in Chicago, Los Angeles, and other cities.

The Patagonian conure has an unusual nesting strategy. In its cold, windy habitat, it makes a den by digging a chamber with a long tunnel. Other conures, like the Nanday, nest in populated areas on fenceposts, unbothered by human activities nearby.

Since macaws live 40 years or more, they are particular about finding the right mate. Young macaw males display for females, hanging upside down and showing off their plumage. It may take a year or two of play and display before one macaw bonds with another.

Macaws, especially the larger species, are slow to reproduce. For starters, they don't always breed yearly. Even when they do, their success rate is low. In a group of 100 breeding pairs, as few as eight chicks may be born each year. These lucky few may spend up to a year being looked after by their parents.

Unlike other parrots, macaws refuse to nest any old where. Often there is competition for suitable spots. The hyacinth macaw chooses burrows on high cliffs; other species demand tree hollows that

►A blue and yellow macaw (*Ara ararauna*) parent guards its nest in the stump of a palm tree. Its mate is away, hunting food for the chick that hides deep within the hollow. Soon it will return and the other macaw will forage.

are high, dry, and predator-safe. Their choosiness is understandable. Hungry snakes, monkeys, and other birds hunt their eggs and chicks. Parasites, birds of prey, and false vampire bats can kill macaw chicks—and on occasion, their parents.

Macaws are devoted parents, feeding their offspring, usually an only child, from their crops. They also supply clay to their chick. Juveniles stay with their indulgent parents for long periods of time, becoming talented whiners. Parents continue to bring food to juveniles long after they've learned to forage for themselves.

Saving our parrots in the wild

Nearly 2,400 years ago, Alexander the Great reached India with his armies, bringing back the first parrots to Europe. For a long time, people believed all parrots came from India. These likeable birds were seen as trophies or entertainment—even more so when taught to talk.

In 1492, when Christopher Columbus first landed in the New World, he spotted parrots on a Caribbean island. The explorer was overjoyed: here was noisy, living proof that he'd found India! To convince his royal backers, Columbus brought 40 parrots to his Spanish queen.

Over the next 500 years, explorers and traders visited these islands, killing or carrying away parrots for their feathers. Pirates and sailors captured them as pets. Locals shot them for food. On some Caribbean islands, parrot numbers shrank to dangerously low levels.

After Captain Cook and others explored Australia and the South Pacific, the budgerigars they brought back found an eager audience in Europe. By the mid-1800s, these small, easily tamed birds became popular with the public. France alone imported 100,000 breeding pairs in a year.

That interest in colorful, talkative birds has led to today's international pet trade in parrots. Although budgies and cockatiels continue to be popular, larger parrots are much in demand. Unlike smaller birds, these species breed slowly and can't replace population losses.

◄ The harsh, laughing calls of the thick-billed parrot (*Rhynchopsitta pachyrhyncha*) used to ring through pine forests in Arizona and New Mexico. Not any more. Logging has wiped out much of their habitat. The birds often nest in pines, and breed when the pinecone seeds ripen. Conservation efforts to save this parrot continue in northern Mexico.

▲ With great care, a researcher at the Tambopata Research Center in Peru measures and weighs a month-old scarlet macaw chick *(Ara macao)* before returning the bird to its nest. Colorful pinfeathers give a hint of the glory the chick will wear as an adult macaw.

Although the United States banned the importation of all wild birds in 1993, illegal trade in parrots continues. The European Union and Asia still allow legal imports. Worldwide, the exotic parrot business, especially for rarer species, is booming.

Plenty of parrot owners cherish their birds. But far too many people buy birds for the wrong reasons: on a whim, as a trophy, as an easy-care investment. A parrot isn't easy to care for, no matter what the ads promise. It requires a varied diet,

►The kea *(Nestor notabilis)* is a curious parrot of the New Zealand mountains. It gives a call that sounds like its name, and builds its nest among the rocks. It even plays in snow. The kea eats almost anything, from roots to insects to carrion or dead animals. Ranchers used to think that keas were pests and killed many of them; the birds are now protected.

not the high-fat seeds many pets are given. A parrot has urgent needs to communicate and explore its surroundings, often by chewing them. Some owners let these bright birds live out their years in solitude, then abandon or sell them because they're a noisy, messy handful.

In countries with few jobs and much poverty, people become parrot poachers to make a living. When poachers trap a macaw chick, they often cut down the nesting tree to get to it, leaving one less place for adult macaws to breed. Many birds are killed while being captured; even more die in transit or quarantine. Countless parrots lose their lives just to get one wild-caught parrot to a dealer.

Habitat loss is the other great destroyer. Logging, mining, farming, and cattle ranching have gobbled up millions of acres of prime parrot habitat. From the Amazon to southeast Asia, parrots and other creatures have lost out to ever-expanding human activity.

These factors have put great pressure on wild parrot populations. Over 90 species, including most of the large macaws, the salmon-crested cockatoo, and the Imperial Amazon parrot, are officially listed as threatened, endangered, or vulnerable.

How can we save these brainy, beautiful birds from extinction? By joining and supporting global conservation efforts of groups like Audubon, Birdlife International, Parrots International, World Parrot Trust, and the Alex Foundation.

Education is another key. On the Caribbean island of St. Lucia, the local parrot was nearly wiped out in the wild until the government partnered with Wildlife Preservation Trust. They set up a reserve, replanted habitat, and gave local people new pride in their native parrot.

Saving a highly threatened family of birds is hard work. Political leaders have to be knowledgeable in order to pass laws and demand enforcement. Parrot rescue takes an informed public. Better education about the lifetime commitment to parrots needs to reach potential owners. African Grey parrots, Amazons, macaws, and cockatoos often live longer than their owners. Even lovebirds and cockatiels can reach 30 years in captivity.

University projects and scientific field studies allow volunteers like me to help in meaningful ways. For instance, the Earthwatch Institute sponsors projects around the world, from rainforest reforestation to the studies run by Dr. Donald Brightsmith in the Tambopata Reserve of Peru. His data on macaw and parrot nesting sites, diet, and clay lick activity is critical for the conservation of macaw populations and the expansion of workable ecotourism in Peru and beyond.

In Central and South America, ecolodges and ecotourism offer promise. If done with respect for local wildlife and people, ecotourism can bring honorable employment and much-needed resources to the original caretakers of the rainforest, while saving parrots.

Fifty years from now, will this planet still be a good home to scarlet macaws and palm cockatoos? Let's hope so. But we need to do more than hope. The parrot family needs protective actions, not just fond wishes and words.

Parrots and their primary habitat, the rainforest, represent a living rainbow of biodiversity. They must not be allowed to vanish. Extinction is a price everyone pays—a price no one can afford.

▶ A giant in every way, the hyacinth macaw of Brazil *(Anodorhynchus hyacinthinus)* has a huge beak, a long tail, and a big head. Hyacinths screech, growl, yap, and make other strange noises. Their beauty has made them hunted and rare. They live on palm nuts, often cracking them on the ground. The hyacinth macaw is a night owl. It stays up on moonlit nights instead of going to sleep at dusk like other parrots.

- African Grey parrots don't just "parrot" words—scientists have proven that they communicate as well as dolphins and gorillas.

- To raise chicks, some parrots borrow termite mounds. If the termites are still home, the insects build a privacy wall between themselves and the nesting birds.

- Bold and hardy parrots called keas live among New Zealand mountains and enjoy playing in snow.

- Macaws give rough cawing cries. The red-necked Amazon makes a call like squeaky brakes. But the sulfur-crested cockatoo is the loudest. It sounds like a car alarm!

- The feet of a hanging parrot grip so well that it can dangle upside-down, sleeping the night away.

- Macaws in Peru, cockatoos in New Guinea, and Grey parrots in Africa all eat clay after meals. Clay gives them salt—and protects them from poisons in the unripe seeds and fruits they eat.

- Only a few predators hunt larger parrots. One is the hawk. The creepiest killer is the false vampire bat. It has a 3-foot wingspan and locates wild parrots while they sleep.

- Some parakeets, cockatoos, and conures glow in the dark. Under ultraviolet light, their feathers have a rare yellow pigment that fluoresces.

- When the hyacinth macaw chomps down on something—hopefully not your finger—it exerts up to 500 pounds of biting pressure per square inch.

- Like humans, parrots favor one limb over the other to hold food. Instead of being right or left-handed, parrots are right- or left-footed.

◄ Pale blue eye-rings and huge head feathers make the white cockatoo (*Cacatua alba*) a standout. When fearful, it raises its tall crest and hisses in alarm. This large bird lives high in the forest trees on Indonesian islands, foraging for fruit and nuts. At dusk, they gather in big groups before roosting.

Glossary

Budgerigar. A small Australian parrot, usually called a parakeet in the United States. The world's most popular bird pet.

Cheek patches. Areas of bare skin of the heads of certain species of macaws and cockatoos. When some species get afraid, angry, or excited, the patches may blush or turn pink.

Collpas. "Place of the salty earth," the Quechua Indian name given to the clay lick areas in Peru and elsewhere in South America, where many species of macaws, parrots, and parakeets come to eat. Clay has salt and protects the birds from the poisonous seeds and plants they sometimes eat.

Crop. A large pouch in the throat of birds, including parrots. In it, both males and females store food for their young. In the crop, hard foods like seeds are softened and somewhat pre-digested.

Eye-blazing. A behavior where the colored irises of a parrot switch from big to small very rapidly. It shows strong emotion. Many species, from small parakeets to large macaws, eye blaze.

Fledge. To be able to fly. A fledgling is a young bird that has just taken its first flight, on its way to becoming an adult.

Fovea. The center of a parrot's eye, the area of sharpest vision. A parrot often cocks its head to aim the fovea toward an object.

Huddle species. Describes social birds that prefer physical contact, especially among mated pairs. Most parrots are huddle species.

Molt. The annual loss and replacement of a bird's feathers. Most parrots molt gradually. With the first molt, juvenile birds take on the coloring and markings of their parents.

Powder down. Specialized feathers of cockatoos that produce a fine dust. Using their bills, cockatoos rub the powdery dust into their plumage, making it soft, fluffy, and sweet-smelling.

Plumage. Refers to all of the feathers of a bird.

Preening. The act of grooming, as most parrots do to each other daily. Parrots use their bills and oil from a preening gland to groom. Preening removes parasites, dead skin, and itchy sheaths on new feathers that come in as the bird molts.

Raptor. A bird of prey, such as a hawk or eagle.

Sentinel bird. Among parrots, one bird that keeps watch while others in the flock feed. It sounds an alarm in case of danger. Parrots take turns being sentinel.

Zygodactylous. A word that describes the four-toed feet of parrots, where two toes point forward and two point the opposite way.

▲ The crimson rosella (*Platycercus elegans*) lives in wooded hills up to the snowline in Australia's mountains. Young rosellas do not resemble their parents until they reach 15 months, when they get their cheerful red feathers.

About the author

Vicki León has written 31 books, including titles for this series on orcas, sea otters, tidepools, wetlands, and octopuses.

Photographers

Outstanding images from 25 wildlife photographers appear on these pages, including principal photographer Clayton Fogle's front cover photo of blue and yellow macaws. R.H. Armstrong/Animals Animals, p. 21; Stanley Breeden/DRK Photo, pp 19, 34; Dr. Donald Brightsmith, pp 6-7, 8-9, 14, 37; Jane Burton/Bruce Coleman Inc, p. 12; John Chellman/Animals Animals, pp 13, 33; Ralph A. Clevenger, pp 27 bottom, 45; E.R. Degginger/Animals Animals, p. 32; Michael Dick/Animals Animals, p. 26; Clayton Fogle, front cover, pp 24, 25, 28 right, 35, 38; Richard R. Hansen, pp 23, 44; Noah Hawthorne, pp 4-5; R.F. Head/Animals Animals, p. 22; Kevin Horan, p. 28 left; M.P. Kahl/DRK Photo, pp 20, 27 top; Zig Leszczynski/Animals Animals, p. 43; Tom Mangelsen, p. 11; C. Allan Morgan, p. 30; Oxford Scientific Films/Animals Animals, p. 18; Robert Pearcy/Animals Animals p. 1; Fritz Prenzel/Animals Animals, back cover, pp 10, 16-17; George Schaller/Bruce Coleman Inc, p. 41; Stan Thompson, p. 40; Rod Williams/Bruce Coleman Inc, p. 36; Art Wolfe, p. 15; Belinda Wright/DRK Photo, p. 47.

Special thanks

- Dr. Donald Brightsmith, project director at Tambopata Research Center and principal investigator for Earthwatch project at TRC
- Geraldine, Aleyda, Daphne, and all the hardworking researchers, guides, and staff at Tambopata Research Center
- Ethologist Dr. Irene Pepperberg; her subject Alex; and her research assistant Robyn Bright
- Marci Hawthorne, wildlife artist
- Noah Hawthorne, photographer and researcher at the Tambopata Research Center
- The helpful staff of the Morro Bay Library
- Tani Smida, California parrot breeder
- Mark Stafford, the Parrot Project
- Richard R. Hansen and Clayton Fogle, wildlife photographers
- Sally Blanchard, avian consultant
- Jay Beckerman, National Parrot Association Director
- Pamela Higdon, Bird Talk magazine
- Mary de Rosa, Animal Kingdom magazine
- Wendy Worth, Bird Department, the Bronx Zoo
- Chris Lazarus, RareFinds
- Robin Maxwell, author and parrot trainer

Where to see parrots

- **Visit zoos, parks, & reserves.**
  A partial list in the U.S. includes:
  Albuquerque Zoo NM; Arizona-Sonora Desert Museum in Tucson AZ; Audubon Park Zoo, New Orleans LA; Baltimore Zoo, MD; Brookfield Zoo, Chicago IL; Busch Gardens, FL; Denver Zoo CO; Houston Zoo TX; Los Angeles Zoo CA; Milwaukee Zooq WI; Bronx Zoo, NY; Parrot Jungle & Gardens, Miami FL; St. Louis Zoo MO; San Antonio Zoo, TX; San Diego Zoo and San Diego Wild Animal Park, CA: San Francisco Zoo, CA; Santa Barbara Zoo, CA; Sea World, CA; Woodland Park Zoo, Seattle WA.

  Outside the U.S.:
  Albuquerque Zoo NM; Arizona-Sonora Desert Museum in Tucson AZ; Audubon Park Zoo, New Orleans LA; Baltimore Zoo, MD; Brookfield Zoo, Chicago IL; Busch Gardens, FL; Denver Zoo CO; Houston Zoo TX; Los Angeles Zoo CA; Milwaukee Zooq WI; Bronx Zoo, NY; Parrot Jungle & Gardens, Miami FL; St. Louis Zoo MO; San Antonio Zoo, TX; San Diego Zoo and San Diego Wild Animal Park, CA: San Francisco Zoo, CA; Santa Barbara Zoo, CA; Sea World, CA; Woodland Park Zoo, Seattle WA.

- **Visit real rainforests & other parrot habitats.**
  Central & South America:
  Brazil: the Pantanal region; the Rio Negro area; Parrot Island, Oriole Island, and Marajo Island; Planalto; jungle excursions from Belem and Manaus.
  Colombia: Leticia and Monkey Islands in the Amazon basin; Tairona National Park.
  Costa Rica: Corocovada and Carara National Parks.
  Ecuador: Napao River region.
  Panama: National Monument Barro Colorado; Coiba Island, Cerro Hoya, and Darien National Parks; and the Metro Natural Park in Panama City.
  Peru: the 50,000 square miles of the Tambopata-Candamo Reserved Zone, on the eastern edge of the Amazon basin; and Manu Biosphere Reserve, about 200 miles northwest of Tambopata.
  Suriname: Foengoe Island near Paramaribo; nature preserves at Brownsberg, Raleigh Falls, Voltzberg, and Wia-Wia.
  Venezuela: Canaima National Park, Orchid Island, Llanos
  Australia:
  National Parks of Bunya Mountain, Hattah Lakes, Blue Mountains, Little Desert, Kakadu, Wyperfield, and Lamington; the Currumbin Bird Sanctuary, Queensland; Ayers Rock and Alice Springs; and in park areas of Brisbane, Cairns, Darwin, Perth.
  New Zealand:
  South Island, Kapiti Island, Arthur's Pass National Park, and Sinbad Valley.

- **Go on real-life scientific expeditions.** Earthwatch Institute has projects on parrots, macaws, and their habitats. Kids 16 and up can take part; scholarships and teacher programs. (www.earthwatch.org)

- **Eavesdrop on wild parrots through an "electronic field trip."** The Jason Project lets students see and hear research in various rainforests, in real time. (www.jasonproject.org)

Helping organizations and good websites

- World Parrot Trust, sponsors of World Parrot Day, work to halt European Union imports of wild-caught birds. With Parrots International, they fund local groups like the Hyacinth Macaw Project and Project Birdwatch, aiding the salmon-crested cockatoo through the harvest and sale of Molucca nuts. (www.worldparrottrust.org)
- Parrots International supports numerous parrot conservation projects, including the Bahaman Amazon, the Puerto Rican parrot recovery program, and Projecto Ara Azul in Brazil's Pantanal. (www.parrotsinternational.org)
- Birdlife International sponsors global conferences, publishes a useful State of the World's Birds each year, available as a download from their site: (www.birdlifeinternational.org)

▲ The ecosystem of the tropical
rainforest, and the macaw species
living in it, are endangered by global
warming and human activities.
Logging hurts the rainforest. It also
hurts macaws, because they use the
biggest, oldest trees for nesting.

- Earthwatch Institute, 3 Clock Tower Place, #100, Maynard MA 01754. Download super info and their catalog on the web: (www.earthwatch.org)
- Tropical Nature Conservation System partners with non-profits in South America on a network of eco-lodges in Peru, Brazil, Ecuador, and Bolivia. (www.tropicalnature.org)
- The Rare Species Conservatory Foundation provides feathered facts and other easy-to-read info on parrots as well as other bird families. (www.rarespecies.org)
- The Alex Foundation continues to support the pioneering work of Dr. Irene Pepperberg on parrot language and intelligence. (www.alexfoundation.org)
- PeruNature partners with the Wildlife Conservation Society, Earthwatch and others. Its website is extremely rich, full of the latest field research done on clay licks, nesting activity, parrots, macaws, and other topics in huge Peruvian reserve called Tambopata-Candamo. (www.perunature.com)
- Duke University hosts the best macaw webpages, its material supplied by Dr. Don Brightsmith, director of the Tambopata Research Center. Besides scientific papers, the site has many downloadable magazine articles in simple language, written by Dr. Brightsmith—making this an excellent site for kids ten and up. (www.duke.edu/~djb4/)
- To learn about non-native parrot flocks that have established themselves in San Francisco and other cities, visit the website of author/photographer Mark Bittner, the protagonist (along with a flock of conures) of the prize-winning film, "The Wild Birds of Telegraph Hill." (www.wildparrotsbook.com)

To learn more

Books

- *Parrots of the World,* by Tony Juniper & Mike Parr. (Yale University Press 1998). A serious and weighty book that covers the parrot family, bird by bird, in 584 pages. The 88 color plates deliver the goods but lack personality somewhat.
- *Wild Parrots of Telegraph Hill,* by Mark Bittner. (Harmony Books 2004). Companion to the hit film of the same name; an insightful book about the behaviors, interactions, and personalities of small fiesty parrots in the conure family.
- *The Alex Studies,* by Dr. Irene Pepperberg. (Harvard U. Press 2000). An invaluable book on the decades of research done by Dr. Pepperberg on the cognitive and communication abilities of Grey parrots. Features her main subject, Alex the Grey parrot.
- *Alex and Friends,* by Dorothy Patent. (Lerner Books 1998). YA book on Alex the Grey parrot, the subject of so much study.
- *The Parrot Action Plan,* published by the IUCN and World Parrot Trust, available through them. Good handbook on parrot conservation.

Magazines

- "Macaws: Winged Rainbows." By Charles Munn. *National Geographic magazine,* January 1994 issue. Although much of the field information is no longer current, the photos by Frans Lanting still stir hearts.

Audio

- The British Parrot Society has a wondrous array of macaw, cockatoo, and parrot sounds in the wild on its website. (www.theparrotsocietyuk.org)

DVDs, videos, & television films

- "The Real Macaw." Granada Wild/Thirteen/WNET New York 2004 VHS format. 60 minutes. Great footage of wild birds, from young scarlet macaws showing off to win mates, chicks in the nest, mealy parrots at the clay lick, blue and yellow macaws in flight. Also shows aspects of trapping by poachers and efforts to eliminate this from the parrot trade.
- "Where the Wild Greys Are." World Parrot Trust 2003. Short DVD with marvelous footage of an African waterhole where flocks of African Greys mingle with forest elephants, plus a second segment on the extinction of the glaucous macaw. Proceeds go to parrot conservation.
- "PollyVision: Strictly for Parrots," World Parrot Trust 2004. 80-minute DVD, an amazing collage of wild birds and behaviors, from duck-waddling galahs to long sequences of parrots and macaws on clay licks. No voice-overs, just wilderness sounds and vocalizations from cockatoos, green Amazons, king parrots, African Greys, hyacinth macaws as they forage, fly, squabble, and groom. Developed to enrich caged parrots' lives but just as fascinating for human viewers.
- "Parrots: Look Who's Talking," a PBS Nature film that reruns periodically on television. A good look and listen at parrot vocalizations, including parrot songsters.
- "Parrots in the Wild," a 3-volume series of DVDs put out by Parrots International. Programs 23–45 minutes-long show great footage of a variety of wild parrots and macaws.

Index

Photographs are numbered in **boldface** and follow the print references after **PP** (photo page).